CELEBRATE
EASTER

52 FUN ACTIVITIES AND DEVOTIONS FOR KIDS

BroadStreet
KIDS

BroadStreet Kids
Savage, Minnesota, USA

BroadStreet Kids is an imprint of BroadStreet Publishing Group, LLC.
Broadstreetpublishing.com

CELEBRATE EASTER

© 2019 by BroadStreet Publishing®
ISBN 978-1-4245-5838-4

Design by Chris Garborg | garborgdesign.com
Created, edited, and compiled by Michelle Winger | literallyprecise.com
Mazes licensed from mazegenerator.net.

Printed in China.

19 20 21 22 23 24 25   7 6 5 4 3 2 1

ALL PROMISES KEPT

You believe in God through Christ.
God raised Christ from death and gave him glory.
So your faith and your hope are in God.
1 PETER 1:21 ICB

We trust God and put our hope in him because what he promises us is true. When Jesus rose again after dying on the cross, he gave us hope forever.

Jesus promised that he would rise from the dead, and he did. Now we know that every other promise he makes is true.

Holy God, I trust that you keep
all your promises and I will always
have hope because of you.

FIND THESE WORDS

ALIVE
CROSS
FREEDOM
GLORY
GRAVE
HOPE
KING
LIFE
POWER
REJOICE
RESURRECTION
RISEN
SACRIFICE
SALVATION
SAVIOR

```
            E V S E P
            M P S O S
            O C O H R
            D R R H E
            O S C Z W
N Y G N M A P X U I J M B E S
E B J L L V H N R E W O P F M
S X D L O D L Y I K B F L I C
I R E S U R R E C T I O N L K
R K D M V K Y K I N G C T J L
            E T E P O
            E V C T F
            K W I K R
            S E O L S
            A C J P A
            L H E I V
            V K R U I
            A G E O O
            T J C U R
            I Y I Q Z
            O N F H G
            N G I L M
            D S R L O
            X I C G D
            T X A V E
            T V S E E
            J M G T R
            C M G Y F
            E V A R G
            S D R K Q
```

5

It Is Finished

After Jesus drank he said, "It is finished."
Then he bowed his head and died.
JOHN 19:30 NIRV

When Jesus died on the cross it would have been a sad day. But when Jesus said, "It is finished," he didn't mean that it was the end. He meant it in the same way you would finish coloring a picture and say, "It is finished."

Jesus completed God's plan for rescuing us. He did this by dying on the cross and then coming alive again a few days later. Jesus finished the job and now we get to have eternal life.

Thank you, Lord, that your finished work on the cross has given me eternal life.

WORD SCRAMBLE

Unscramble the letters to discover common colors.

UPELRP _ _ _ _ _ _

NPIK _ _ _ _

ENGER _ _ _ _ _

LWLEOY _ _ _ _ _ _

ERAOGN _ _ _ _ _ _

ERD _ _ _

UBLE _ _ _ _

WBONR _ _ _ _ _

CALBK _ _ _ _ _

THEWI _ _ _ _ _

Answer on page 124

7

Sacrifice of Praise

Bring your petition. Come to the Lord and say,
"O Lord, take away our sins;
be gracious to us and receive us,
and we will offer you the sacrifice of praise."
HOSEA 14:2 TLB

Have you ever had to share your favorite toy or game with your little brother, sister, or friend that has come to stay? A sacrifice is giving up something that you really like for someone or something else.

When you have done something wrong, the Bible says to ask God to take away your sin and then to praise him for being good to you. This is your sacrifice for God: saying wonderful things about him, even when you don't feel wonderful.

God, you deserve to hear me say great things about you. Thank you for forgiving me when I say that I am sorry.

COLLECT ALL THE BUNNIES!

Draw a line from the beginning to the end that passes through each box with a bunny in it once. The line can go up, down, left, or right, but cannot go diagonal.

Start here ➡

➡ **End here**

ETERNAL LIFE

These children are people with physical bodies. So Jesus himself became like them and had the same experiences they have. He did this so that, by dying, he could destroy the one who has the power of death. That one is the devil. Jesus became like men and died so that he could free them. They were like slaves all their lives because of their fear of death.
HEBREWS 2:14-15 ICB

Have you ever been losing a game and then someone says that they would like to start the game again? It's like you've been given a second chance to win!

Jesus died on the cross, but then he rose again, which means he came back to life! Jesus did this to show us that even though we will die one day, we will also live again, just like he did. Don't be afraid, you have been given eternal life!

Jesus, thank you that you beat death and gave me eternal life.

Recreate the picture above in the grid below.

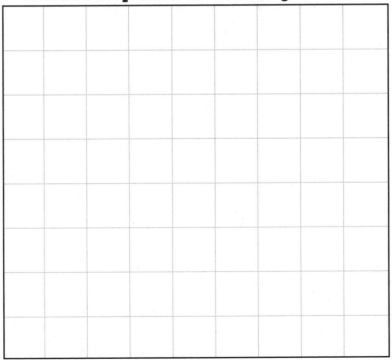

Circle the 10 differences between these 2 pictures, and then color!

JOYFUL MUSIC

During danger he will keep me safe in his shelter.
He will hide me in his Holy Tent.
Or he will keep me safe on a high mountain.
My head is higher than my enemies around me.
I will offer joyful sacrifices in his Holy Tent.
I will sing and praise the Lord.
Lord, hear me when I call.
Be kind and answer me.

PSALM 27:5-7 ICB

Do you play an instrument, or would you like to play an instrument? What kind of music do you like to listen to? Each of us were given the gift of either making music or enjoying it.

God gave us music as a gift, it can help us in times of trouble. When we feel annoyed, sad, or upset, music can help bring joy to your heart. The next time you feel like you might get into trouble with your attitude, give it to God and play some music. Let his gift of music help you find joy.

Jesus, when times are hard, help me to choose joy again and again. Let the joy that you give me be a witness and a testimony to the love you have for me.

Circle the two pictures that are exactly the same.

Answer on page 124

PATH TO PEACE

*Those who love your teachings will find true peace.
Nothing will defeat them.*
PSALM 119:165 ICB

Have you ever wanted to cheat on a game so you could win? Or cross the road in the wrong place just to get to the other side quicker? Maybe you won't wear a helmet because you think it looks silly. Following rules is sometimes hard!

God made up some rules—not to make it hard for you, but to keep you safe, and keep others safe around you. When you love God's rules, it means that you trust that he knows what is best for you, and that gives you a lot of peace!

Lord, I want to please you and keep your rules because I know that I will be a more peaceful person when I live by your goodness.

Start
here

A Beautiful Sound

To choose life is to love the LORD your God, obey him, and stay close to him. He is your life, and he will let you live many years in the land, the land he promised to give your ancestors Abraham, Isaac, and Jacob.

DEUTERONOMY 30:20 NCV

Do your parents still tell you to stay close to them when you cross the road? Maybe they make you hold their hand. The reason they do this is because they want to protect you from the dangers of a busy road. They want to keep you safe.

God wants to keep you safe, too. That's why he says to stay close to him. He wants you to live a long happy life, just like he has promised other friends of his, like Abraham, Isaac, and Jacob.

Father, thank you for keeping me safe. Help me to stay close by your side so that I can live a great life.

**Write down a word in each of the blanks below.
Use your words to create a new story.**

1. _____ Adjective

2. _____ Noun (plural)

3. _____ Noun (plural)

4. _____ Noun (plural)

5. _____ Noun

6. _____ Verb

7. _____ Noun (plural)

8. _____ Verb (+ING)

9. _____ Verb (+ING)

10. _____ Verb

11. _____ Animal (plural)

12. _____ Verb

13. _____ Noun (plural)

14. _____ Activity

15. _____ Adjective

16. _____ Adjective

17. _____ Adjective

18. _____ Verb

SPRING IS HERE!

In the spring, there are a lot of __1__ things happening. Leaves bud on __2__ , __3__ grow out of the ground, and chicks hatch from their __4__ . The sun begins to warm up the __5__ and all traces of snow __6__ away.

Kids can be seen riding __7__ , __8__ at parks, and __9__ butterflies. After being cooped up all winter, it's finally time to __10__ . __11__ must be the most excited of all. They __12__ on their leashes, and beg their owners to throw __13__ , over and over again.

But, one of the best things to do in the spring is __14__ . It makes people feel __15__ and __16__ .

Spring is really the most __17__ time of the year! So, get outside and __18__ .

SIGNS

"Stand where the roads cross and look.
Ask where the old way is.
Ask where the good way is, and walk on it.
If you do, you will find rest for yourselves.
But you have said, 'We will not walk on the good way!'
JEREMIAH 6:16 ICB

If you go for a drive, or even out for a walk, you will see a lot of signs. Signs point you to the way that you want to go, and they tell you about the place you just passed. If you see a food sign, you know there is food inside. If you see a sign that says, "Do not enter," you know that you can't go there.

When you have decisions to make, like whether to practice your instrument or play a game, think about the kinds of signs that God gives you. Would he say no or yes? Would he say, "This is good," or, "This is bad." Learn God's ways because they are always right.

God, help me to understand and listen to you when I have to make important decisions. I know you will lead me to the right way.

*C*hange one letter at a time to create new words and turn **SINS** into **GIFT**.

S I N S

_ _ _ _ sharp metal objects

_ _ _ _ a type of tree

_ _ _ _ a straight mark

_ _ _ _ bits of thread

_ _ _ _ a series of items

_ _ _ _ the main idea

G I F T

Answer on page 124

DOT SQUARE GAME—PLAY WITH A FRIEND!

Connect two flowers with a line. Take turns connecting flowers.
If you draw a line that completes a box, put your initials in that
box—it's yours! Whenever a player makes a box, they get to take
another turn. At the end of the game, count the boxes with your
initials in it. The player with the most boxes wins!

A Broken Heart

The Lord is close to the brokenhearted.
He saves those whose spirits have been crushed.
PSALM 34:18 ICB

Jesus knows what it's like to have a broken heart. He was hurt by people he cared about and it was hard for him to die on the cross. That's why the Bible says he can be near to us when we are having a hard time because he understands.

Are you having a hard time, today? Do you know someone who is sad, or mad, or upset? Remember that Jesus cares and he will rescue you when you need it the most.

God, I am so grateful that you understand when I have a bad day. Thank you that you are always near me.

```
        H I N I                   W B Y H
      C T F V O H               O L W I X T
    P H M J B Y I X           Y F C B I F E H
  V O V R Z H H B T Z       A C C E P T A N C E
  T M U A C F T Y F A P U O D E E X I D B R
  M V W W S T A T C O M P A S S I O N E Y V
  N O I S S A P I B C L R K I P J N Y R T G
  R R H V I V M N O L C K I P D Z O L N H D
  O L E W B I E A B K N F S F P R I L E L D
    J A Y R N R M J Y O V Y C F U T X S I
    T P V H R O U P N I W M H V A O X S G
      R G O N T H E O T P P K Y E V Z O
      F A I R I P X I A T A X D H E O F
        V E U P I P T R Y T W U S D N
        I H T P B C O S H Q F N K
          M G T A E D W Y H E A
            O P R F A B W S O
            I M F X F S G
              F A E K M
              K S F
              S
```

FIND THESE WORDS

ACCEPTANCE	COMPASSION	HUMANITY
ADORATION	DEVOTION	PASSION
AFFECTION	EMPATHY	SYMPATHY
AFFIRMATION	GOODNESS	TENDERNESS
APPROVAL	HEART	WARMTH

HARD LOVE

We know what love is because Jesus Christ gave his life for us. So we should give our lives for our brothers and sisters.

1 JOHN 3:16 NIRV

It was a hard experience for Jesus to have to die on the cross. It hurt him and made him feel rejected by everyone. He went through this pain because he loves us and he knew that giving us eternal life was going to be the best thing for us.

It would be pretty hard to do what Jesus did, but thankfully he only had to do that once. We don't have to die on a cross, but we do have to love people so much, just like Jesus does.

Thank you, Jesus, for going through such a hard thing, all because you love me. Help me to love others in the same way.

Make new words out of the letters in the word

EASTER.

Each letter should only be used once.

T _ _ _ _ _   E _ _ _   A _ _

T _ _ _ _   R _ _ _   E _ _

T _ _ _ _   R _ _ _   E _ _

R _ _ _ _   R _ _ _   R _ _

R _ _ _ _   S _ _ _   S _ _

S _ _ _ _   S _ _ _   S _ _

S _ _ _ _   S _ _ _   S _ _

A _ _ _   T _ _ _   T _ _

E _ _ _   T _ _ _   T _ _

E _ _ _   T _ _ _   T _ _

Answer on page 125

Gift of Faithfulness

*"I have brought you glory on earth
by finishing the work you gave me to do."*
John 17:4 NIV

You know when you have been asked to do a task, like your homework, or clearing away the dishes? It feels good to finish something that you knew you were supposed to do. Faithfulness is all about sticking to what you said you were going to do.

Jesus had to be faithful as well. Going to the cross was not an easy thing for him to finish, but he knew that it was God's plan. So, he finished the task that God gave him. Because of his faithfulness, we now have eternal life with him.

Jesus, thank you so much for finishing the work you had to do on the cross. Your faithfulness is a gift to me.

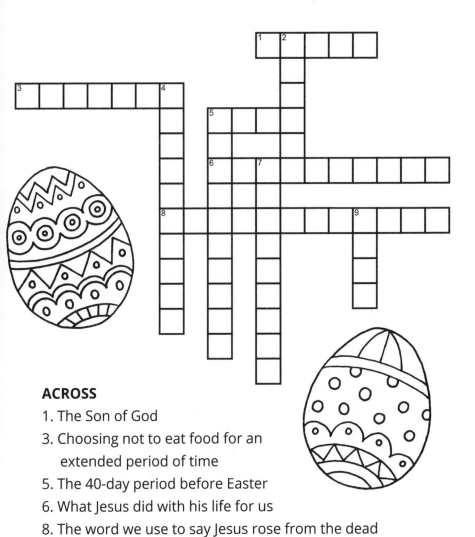

ACROSS

1. The Son of God
3. Choosing not to eat food for an extended period of time
5. The 40-day period before Easter
6. What Jesus did with his life for us
8. The word we use to say Jesus rose from the dead

DOWN

2. An important holiday in Christianity
4. The day Jesus hung on the cross (2 words, 4-6)
5. When Jesus presented the first communion (2 words, 4-6)
7. Someone who follows the teachings of Jesus
9. The place where Jesus' body was laid

Answer on page 125

Best Outfit

You are God's chosen people. You are holy and dearly loved. So put on tender mercy and kindness as if they were your clothes. Don't be proud. Be gentle and patient.
Colossians 3:12 nirv

What is your favorite thing to wear? Is it a certain jacket, or sports shirt? Maybe you enjoy dressing up in a costume, or maybe you just like wearing your pajamas!

The Bible talks about putting on clothes of kindness and gentleness and patience. What would that look like? We would make a decision to be a kind, gentle, loving person. When we remember to be kind, humble, and gentle we will always feel like we are wearing our best clothes.

Father, help me to remember to dress properly today, putting on good things like kindness, patience, love, and gentleness.

Word Scramble

Unscramble the letters to discover
the names for baby animals.

KHICC _ _ _ _ _ _

NPYO _ _ _ _ _

UPPYP _ _ _ _ _ _

EKTNIT _ _ _ _ _ _ _

WANF _ _ _ _ _

ICDKULGN _ _ _ _ _ _ _ _ _

UBC _ _ _ _

FALC _ _ _ _ _

EPLIGT _ _ _ _ _ _ _

BALM _ _ _ _ _

Answer on page 125

ASK CONFIDENTLY

*Let us come boldly to the very throne of God
and stay there to receive his mercy and to find
grace to help us in our times of need.*
HEBREWS 4:16 TLB

When you don't know how to do something,
what do you do? You can't just sit there and wait
for someone to tell you. You have to go find
somebody who knows and ask them to help you.
Grown-ups love it when you tell them that you
don't quite understand.

God is the same! It gives him joy to be able to
help you when you need it, because he loves you
and he wants what is best for you. Be brave; ask
him for help!

**Lord, thank you for wanting to help me. I
know I can come to you with all my needs.**

Figure out the secret message by using the code.

◎	▲	☼	□	◖	✓	❖	◆	✿	✝	☺	✏	〰
A	B	C	D	E	F	G	H	I	J	K	L	M

★	↑	↓	●	⌘	✾	✂	⁂	▣	✸	✂	※	❄
N	O	P	Q	R	S	T	U	V	W	X	Y	Z

I KNOW THAT

MY REDEEMER LIVES,

AND THAT IN THE END

HE WILL STAND

ON THE EARTH.

JOB

_ ____ ____

__ _____ _____'

___ ____ __ ___ ___

__ ____ _____

__ ___ _____.

___ 19:25

Answer on page 125

A BEAUTIFUL DAY

I will tell about the Lord's kindness.
And I will praise him for what he has done.
He has given many good things to us.
He has been very good to the people of Israel.
The Lord has shown mercy to us.
And he has been kind to us.
ISAIAH 63:7 ESV

God's goodness is great every day; his love is steady and always fights for us. We can show God how thankful we are by remembering how good he is and telling others about what he has done.

Even when life is hard, the list of blessings God has given you is very long. This day is beautiful because God loves you and he is so good to you.

You are so good, God! Thank you for your kindness to me. Help me to share your love with others.

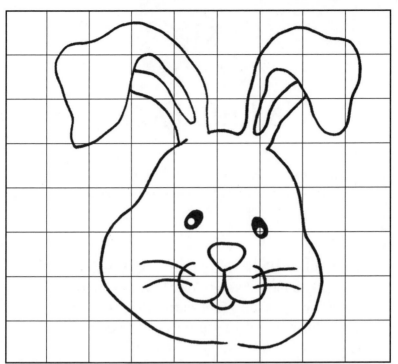

Recreate the picture above in the grid below.

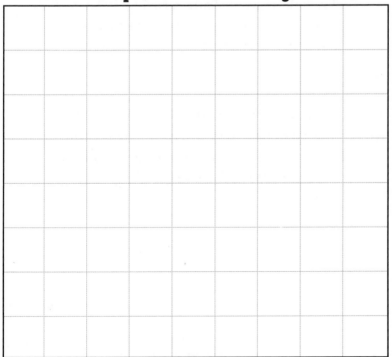

A KIND FACE

Answer me, O LORD, for your steadfast love is good;
according to your abundant mercy, turn to me.
PSALM 69:16 NRSV

What do you think God's face looks like when you talk to him? If you think of God as angry or mean, you probably feel a little afraid of him. If you think of him as a grumbly giant, you may not like him at all.

God is your heavenly Father. He looks like a really kind Dad. He is so happy when you come to talk to him and he wants you to trust him.

Father, thank you that you invite
me to come to you when I need you.
You wait for my steps toward you and
you welcome me with a big hug.

```
          B T T E F S X C
        Y L A R K S P U R F J C
      A I T C Z V O S J P G S N H
    D I X X G M P V Y X Y J P P O N
  G X L H H T N I C A Y H A Q Q A E X
  M Q O N O P H B W G T N S S R E P P
A Z T N D I H C R O X S P M C T Z K Z X
I S X G V V W R Z T Y O H I M M Q S F C
N G P A A L D S B I G C S N X K G R H C
O O R M G W K Z G H D S E E S Y G R E E
G V S P E T U N I A U L W N I C Y T J A
E N M O S T B V J S E T O X U S M Y P D
B B O D Q L A V E N D E R G A K C Z H B
R E H H I D P M K D I A W N I K P A W K
  Z I N N I A Z W H K J T V F R Z Y R
  W Q D X N D O O X P H M R S E A K G
    A I L L E M A C E P X U L C M M
      O A U T S C M C I Z N R C E
        P M Q M U H G G Y M Y W
          K M O S D Y V H
```

FIND THESE WORDS

BEGONIA   JASMINE   NARCISSUS

CAMELLIA   LARKSPUR   ORCHID

CHRYSANTHEMUM   LAVENDER   PANSY

HAZEL   MAGNOLIA   PETUNIA

HYACINTH   MARIGOLD   ZINNIA

ENDLESS LOVE

The Lord shows mercy and is kind.
He does not become angry quickly,
and he has great love.
PSALM 103:8 ICB

You know when you have done something wrong and you think your parents are going to yell at you? You expected them to be angry, but instead they treated you kindly.

God has that kind of love for you. He is full of mercy and grace, which means that he is kind to you even when you have done something wrong. He doesn't get angry quickly and he makes sure that you know of his great love.

Father, thank you for your love. Help me do the right thing even though I know you will show me kindness no matter what.

Find your way to the Easter egg!

Start here

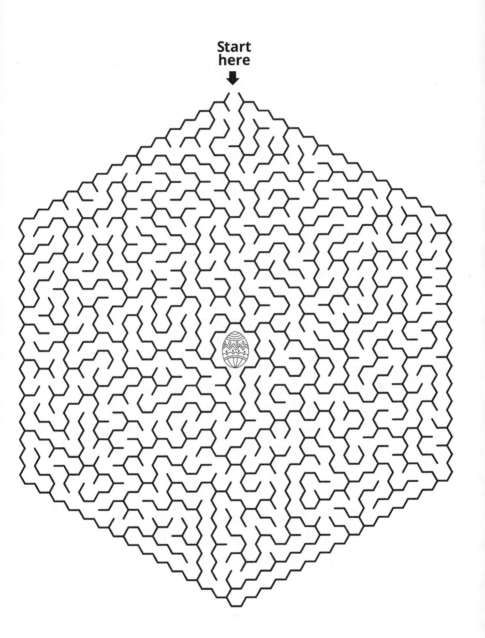

Getting Dressed

God has chosen you and made you his holy people. He loves you. So you should always clothe yourselves with mercy, kindness, humility, gentleness, and patience.

COLOSSIANS 3:12 NCV

Every day when you step out of bed, you have a choice to make. Am I going to be happy or sad? Nice or mean? Positive or negative?

God tells us to pick out our attitude like we pick out our clothes. We do not have to always pretend like we are the happiest person in the world, but even on bad days we have a choice. You could be the person that brightens someone's day by giving them a little taste of the joy you have found in Jesus.

Father God, today I ask that you help me choose to have a better mood and make good choices for you.

Circle the two pictures that are exactly the same.

Answer on page 125

God of All Comfort

Praise be to the God and Father of our Lord Jesus Christ. God is the Father who is full of mercy. And he is the God of all comfort.
2 Corinthians 1:3 icb

Comfort is what we need when sad things happen. We need someone to sit beside us, listen to our story, and give us a big hug. Sometimes we don't have friends and family right next to us but remember that God is there. You can talk to him whenever you feel like it.

Have a great day today. You have a God who loves you. He cares about you. Let him help you when you are down.

Father, I give you my worry and ask that you would hold my heart. I begin this day with you right next to me.

COLLECT ALL THE CHICKS!

Draw a line from the beginning to the end that passes through each box with a chick in it once. The line can go up, down, left, or right, but cannot go diagonal.

Start here ⬇

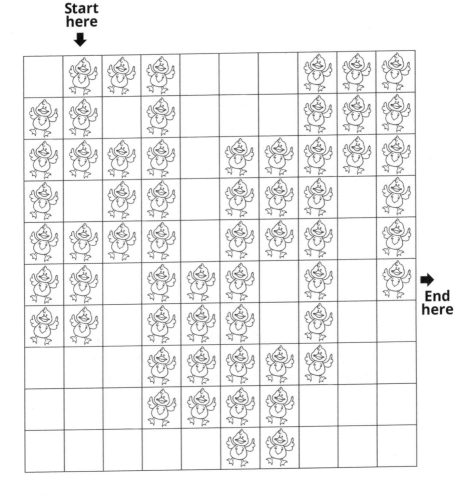

➡ **End here**

No Conditions

Let us, then, feel free to come before God's throne. Here there is grace. And we can receive mercy and grace to help us when we need it.
HEBREWS 4:16 ICB

It is hard to believe that love will remain forever. The love that God the Father has for us comes without rules. There is absolutely nothing we can do or say that will take away his love.

Even though we sometimes make bad choices, we can still go to God for forgiveness. He will always welcome us when we are sorry. In fact, he says to be bold about asking for forgiveness. Ask him for his grace, and he will say yes!

Thank you, Jesus, that I can be so sure that you will forgive me. I ask for your forgiveness right now and know that you welcome me with love.

Make new words out of the letters in the word
BASKET.

Each letter should only be used once.

B _ _ _ _   S _ _ _ _   T _ _ _

B _ _ _ _   T _ _ _ _   T _ _ _

B _ _ _ _   B _ _ _   S _ _ _

S _ _ _ _   B _ _ _   S _ _ _

S _ _ _ _   B _ _ _   A _ _

                B _ _ _   B _ _

                B _ _ _   B _ _

                B _ _ _   S _ _

                T _ _ _   S _ _

                                   S _ _

                                   T _ _

Answer on page 126

47

MADE CLEAN

O loving and kind God, have mercy. Have pity upon me and take away the awful stain of my transgressions. Oh, wash me, cleanse me from this guilt. Let me be pure again.

PSALM 51:1-2 TLB

Nobody is perfect. We all make mistakes. The really great news is that God loves us all anyway; it doesn't matter what we have done.

King David made some terrible mistakes, probably worse than you would ever make. David knew that he could turn to his Father in heaven and be made clean. We can do the same. Our incredible God shows us grace when we least deserve it. We only need to ask for it.

Lord, I ask for your forgiveness. I ask for my sins to be washed away and for my heart to become clean again.

```
                        M  P  K
                     M  E  L  F  O
                     R  R  C  N  V
                     L  C  H  N  Z
          Y  X  L        I  Y  E  K  G        V  E  V
       H  C  J  J  P     H  A  A  B  F     Z  K  G  I  Q
       E  A  D  R  H  F     H  M  E     R  F  R  Q  O  S
       X  R  P  W  T  M  Y  L  P  T  S  V  A  N  P  I  O
          G  E  U  L  A  V  G  Y  X  Y  C  Q  Q  V  Q
             O  R  K  V  V  C  I  T  E  H  M  D  X
                   E  T  T  I  V  I  Z
             L  W  R  R  X  H  P  V  R  R  P
             U  L  N  M  H  U  E  G  L  Z  A  L  T
          S  A  R  E  J  F     Z     I  C  I  H  H  E
          C  E  Z  G  A  O     J     O  L  X  R  C  S
          R  O  N  O  H        H        W  S  S  L  Q
             F  Q  S           T           A  B  P
                               R
                               O
                               W
                               H
                               E
                               L
                               O
                               V
                               E
                               M
                               W
       E  C  A  E  P  R  Z  V  I  V  S  Y  P  S  I
       V  X  V  F  O  R  G  I  V  E  N  E  S  S  L
       M  C  V  Y  K  F  W  K  H  O  V  P  Y
       P  A  Y  G  I  T  A  K  G  X  A  G  M
       F  J  H  J  N  F  F  P  R  R  T  M  M
       K  X  O  G  D  N  G  K  D  N  Y  A  E
       D  S  B  T  N  O  U  O  G  Y  F  Q  D
          H  I  U  E  J  N  S  L  G  O  D
          T  I  U  S  O  P  D  U  W  Y  P
          G  N  I  S  S  E  L  B  O  H  T
          X  F  J  A  M  D  J  J  P
```

FIND THESE WORDS

BLESSING

CHARITY

FAVOR

FORGIVENESS

GRACE

HONOR

JOY

KINDNESS

LIGHT

LOVE

MERCY

PARDON

PEACE

VALUE

WORTH

Circle the 10 differences between these 2 pictures, and then color!

Loving Right

The Lord wants to show his mercy to you.
He wants to rise and comfort you.
The Lord is a fair God.
And everyone who waits for his help will be happy.
Isaiah 30:18 icb

We all get grumpy sometimes. We shout, we push, we say unkind things. Usually when this happens we get in trouble. This is because adults want you to grow up into a person that treats people with kindness.

God doesn't want us to be mean either, but his first response to your grumpiness is not anger. He wants to show you love even when you have done wrong. When you feel his love, it helps you to be more kind and fair to others.

Jesus, thank you that you show me love and not anger. Help me to be a more kind and fair person because of your love.

Start here

End here

A MILLION PLUS ONE

Praise the Lord!
Thank the Lord because he is good.
His love continues forever.
PSALM 106:1 ICB

Have you ever said, "I forgive you," so many times that you get sick of it? Maybe your brother or sister has annoyed you and then said sorry. You will forgive them, but if they keep doing it, you don't want to forgive them anymore. It's frustrating!

Thankfully, our God doesn't feel like we do about forgiveness. His love for you is so great that he will forgive you every single time that you ask for forgiveness. Even if it is millions of times!

Lord, I am so grateful that you
forgive me every time I ask you to.
Thank you for your mercy.

DESIGN AND COLOR
YOUR OWN EGG

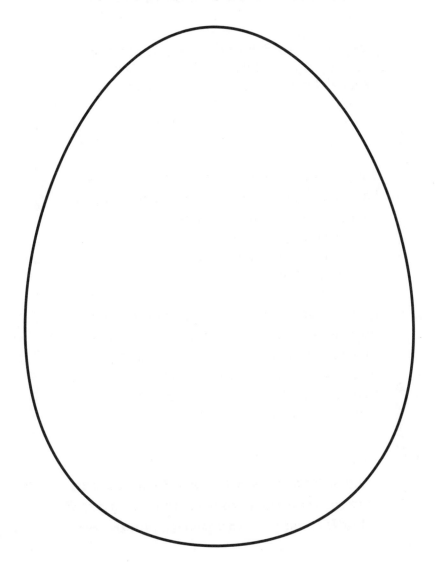

When Life Is Hard

I begged the Lord three times to take this problem away from me. But he said to me, "My grace is enough for you. When you are weak, my power is made perfect in you."
2 Corinthians 12:8-9 NCV

You make the team and then break a bone and have to spend all season on the bench. One of your parents is sick and God is not healing them. Your best friend moves away and now you have to find a new group of friends. What is going on? Does God want you to struggle?

God does not want anyone to be hurt, but he does use hard times to show us his power and make us better people. Maybe losing that friend means you found a great, new group of friends that you have for the rest of your life! God can turn hard things into good things.

Lord God, help me to see that you can use my weakness to do something great. I will trust you and praise you in that.

Break the code to figure out the secret message. Some of the numbers have been provided to help you get started.

12						21	2		13		9
A	B	C	D	E	F	G	H	I	J	K	L	M

			25		20			11	16		26
N	O	P	Q	R	S	T	U	V	W	X	Y	Z

18-5-7 10-5-4 22-5 14-5-3-15-4 20-21-15 11-5-7-14-4

_ _ _   _ _ _   _ _   _ _ _ _ _   _ _ _   _ _ _ _ _

20-21-12-20 21-15 10-12-3-15 21-2-22 5-6-15 12-6-4

_ _ _ _   _ _   _ _ _ _   _ _ _   _ _ _   _ _ _

5-6-14-19 22-5-6 20-21-12-20, 11-21-5-15-3-15-7

_ _ _ _   _ _ _   _ _ _ _   _ _ _ _ _ _ _

17-15-14-2-15-3-15-22 2-6 21-2-9 22-21-12-14-14

_ _ _ _ _ _ _ _   _ _   _ _ _   _ _ _ _ _

6-5-20 23-15-7-2-22-21 17-24-20 21-12-3-15

_ _ _   _ _ _ _ _ _   _ _ _   _ _ _ _

15-20-15-7-6-12-14 14-2-18-15.

_ _ _ _ _ _ _   _ _ _ _.

Answer on page 126

INTIMATE FRIENDSHIP

The grace of the Lord Jesus Christ, the love of God, and the fellowship of the Holy Spirit be with you all.
2 CORINTHIANS 13:14 ICB

What do you like to do with your friends? Do you invite them to your parties? Play games with them? Do you like talking about interesting things with them?

God wants to be your friend! There is a special friendship between God, Jesus, and the Holy Spirit and they want you to join in this friendship. The very best way to be a good friend of God is to talk to him. You don't see God, but he sees you and he cares about everything you have to say!

Lord, you consider me a friend, and I think that's great. Help me to be a good friend to you by talking and listening to you.

USJDA

_ _ _ _ _

TEEPR

_ _ _ _ _

EJUSS

_ _ _ _ _

RAMY ADELMGANE

_ _ _ _   _ _ _ _ _ _ _ _ _

MINOS

_ _ _ _ _

NPTUOIS TAILEP

_ _ _ _ _ _ _ _   _ _ _ _ _ _

ISDLICPSE

_ _ _ _ _ _ _ _ _

HNJO

_ _ _ _

EASPRHISE

_ _ _ _ _ _ _ _

EJAMS

_ _ _ _ _

Answer on page 126

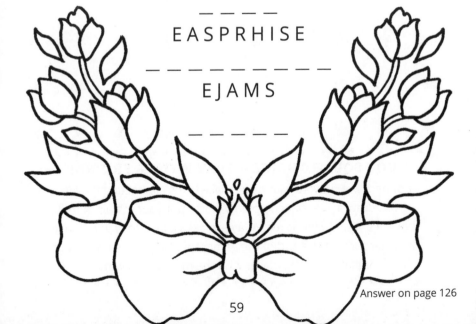

WORD SCRAMBLE

Unscramble the letters to discover the names of people in the Easter story.

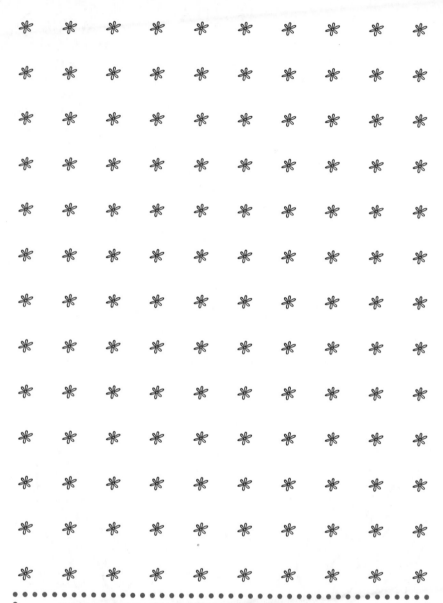

DOT SQUARE GAME—PLAY WITH A FRIEND!

Connect two flowers with a line. Take turns connecting flowers.
If you draw a line that completes a box, put your initials in that
box—it's yours! Whenever a player makes a box, they get to take
another turn. At the end of the game, count the boxes with your
initials in it. The player with the most boxes wins!

Made Right

All need to be made right with God by his grace, which is a free gift. They need to be made free from sin through Jesus Christ. God sent him to die in our place to take away our sins.

Romans 3:24-25 ncv

Sometimes life is hard to understand. But faith is simple. When we put our faith in Jesus, God sees the goodness of Jesus in our lives, not our sin. This is how God is able to forgive us.

When troubles seem overwhelming, you can run straight to God. He gave you the gift of Jesus and everything has been made right.

God, thank you for the free gift of forgiveness through Jesus Christ. I gladly accept your gift!

Write down a word in each of the blanks below.
Use your words to create a new story.

1. _____ Verb
2. _____ Adjective
3. _____ Body part (plural)
4. _____ Verb (+ING)
5. _____ Adjective
6. _____ Place
7. _____ Noun
8. _____ Verb
9. _____ Place
10. _____ Verb (+ING)
11. _____ Animal
12. _____ Verb

13. _____ Noun
14. _____ Noun
15. _____ Number
16. _____ Place
17. _____ Noun
18. _____ Noun
19. _____ Adjective
20. _____ Adjective
21. _____ Noun
22. _____ Verb
23. _____ Verb

AFTER A LONG NAP

I yawn and **1** my **2** furry **3** above my head. I feel like I have been **4** for a very long time and I am **5** ! Finally, it's time for me to come out of my **6** and explore the **7** . I am on the hunt for something to **8** .

My first stop is the **9** . **10** is one of my favorite things to do. I especially like to catch **11** . I see one **12** out of the water and I snatch it out of the **13** . It slips and slides right out of my paws and back into the **14** . That was one lucky fish. The next **15** don't get so lucky.

After spending the morning by the water, I decide it would be fun to see the **16** from a higher view. I climb a **17** . Up, up, up I go until I cannot go any higher. From way up here, I can see the whole **18** . It is **19** . I am so glad this is my home.

My day has been exciting, but I am feeling a little **20** . It must be time for a **21** . Off I head to my cave. But this time I won't **22** for so long. I have a lot to **23** before winter comes back.

THE RIPPLE EFFECT

All of this is for your benefit.
And as God's grace reaches more and more people,
there will be great thanksgiving,
and God will receive more and more glory.
2 CORINTHIANS 4:15 NLT

When you throw a rock into a still pond, what happens? Lots of circles of water start to show up and they get bigger and bigger as they go out. This is what God's grace is like.

When we are given grace, we feel God's love and can't wait to share it with others. Then they share our excitement and also give thanks to God. This is how we can spread the love of God all over the world. Let's give thanks to God!

Gracious God, help me to tell about your goodness to more people. I want everyone to know how great you are!

Start here ↓

BECAUSE OF LOVE

That Christ may dwell in your hearts through faith,
as you are being rooted and grounded in love.
EPHESIANS 3:17 NRSV

As a plant grows, we usually only see what is happening above the dirt. We admire the leaves and the colors of the flowers. But no plant looks like that without some strong, sturdy roots in the soil. Those roots keep the plant growing healthy and beautiful.

We become beautiful people when we let God be like our roots. If you can remind yourself every day that God loves you, you will show his love on the outside and that will make you even more beautiful.

Father, give me the grace to trust your love for me. Help me grow my roots in your love and nothing else.

Write every second letter on the spaces below to reveal the hidden message.

Start
here

__ __ __ __ __ __ __ __ __ __ __;

__ __ __ __ __ __ __ __ __ __!

Luke 24:6

Answer on page 126

READY TO FORGIVE

Be gentle and ready to forgive; never hold grudges. Remember, the Lord forgave you, so you must forgive others.
COLOSSIANS 3:13 TLB

Have you ever had a fight with a friend that lasted for days? It can be pretty sad to be mad at someone for a long time. It doesn't feel great. That's what a grudge is, staying mad, instead of letting go and forgiving.

How do you forgive people? You just do! The Bible doesn't say that there are words that we need to use, or that we have to feel good about someone. It just says to forgive. It starts with saying in your heart, or out loud, that you forgive that person. The cool thing is that Jesus does the rest for you; you just have to let go.

Lord, you have forgiven me. Please give me the grace to forgive those who have done wrongs things to me.

ACROSS

3. A word people used to praise Jesus when he came into Jerusalem
7. The name of the garden where Jesus and his disciples went to pray
8. The disciple who betrayed Jesus
10. The disciple who denied Jesus three times

DOWN

1. The high priest at the time of Jesus' arrest
2. The part of the body cut off a soldier by one of Jesus' disciples
4. The type of food that symbolizes Jesus' body in Communion
5. What the disciples did in the Garden instead of praying
6. What animal Jesus rode into Jerusalem
9. Who told Mary that Jesus was no longer in the tomb

Answer on page 126

THE DO-OVER

The faithful love of the L{ORD} never ends!
His mercies never cease.
Great is his faithfulness;
his mercies begin afresh each morning.
LAMENTATIONS 3:22-23 NLT

Have you ever seen a movie where the person gets to go back in time and do the whole day again? Maybe the person is able to fix a mistake and make everything go the right way.

Living in God's grace is kind of like getting to start over each day. God does not hold anything from yesterday against you. He has new blessings for you each morning.

Jesus, I receive your love and forgiveness this morning. Help me to focus on today and not worry about yesterday.

BRAG ABOUT GOD

He said to me, "My grace is all you need.
My power is strongest when you are weak."
So I am very happy to brag about how weak I am.
Then Christ's power can rest on me.
2 CORINTHIANS 12:9 NIRV

Who would want to brag about being the slowest runner on a race team? Or the worst student? Or the least creative artist? It's not very often that we hear people being proud about what they are bad at. We like to show off our skills.

The Bible thinks of bragging differently. It says that we can brag about what we are not good at. Why would it say that? When we are not very good at something, we can see that God is great. We can say, "Wow, there is no way I could have done that all by myself."

God, shine through the things that I am not good at so I know that you are with me and I can show others how much you care for them.

```
K L K X V P A B Q U Q H A P T O H R N W
A G E M O D N A A H P L A C P A S L B A
R H U S X P S Y Z V X N A S A V I O R E
J H Q D F S F V W P B F B V L A D V G P
I M R Y L W N R E M E E D E R Q R Y Y D
I O G G M R L E U N A M M E A V O A A W
E O W G E O O W J F C Z N X O E L U F R
X R L F N U E W K I N G O F K I N G S E
D G L T H G J C E A R O M J C G E G Y R
C E C H I V X V O H P L O V O S S D H E
O D C F F O G V E C T H A O A M I V E V
L I O N O F J U D A H F T M S A R E H I
A R C L W C U L P C D D O W B S G A I L
P B A Z Q B Q M M J N E T T I O I P B E
G I E U B Z L M D E M I U M H S F B B D
A J E J B N A M F O N O S H S G Q G N P
F W W C V T W N A X G H X E R F I J O Y
N A L M I G H T Y O N E M F O L A L O D
T S O M L H I G O O D S H E P H E R D P
R F V X O S T F E X F X B G Z P L D D W
```

FIND THESE WORDS

ALMIGHTY ONE	GOOD SHEPHERD	MESSIAH
ALPHA AND OMEGA	KING OF KINGS	REDEEMER
BRIDEGROOM	LAMB OF GOD	RISEN LORD
DELIVERER	LIGHT OF THE WORLD	SAVIOR
EMMANUEL	LION OF JUDAH	SON OF MAN

75

I Need Grace

God continues to give us more grace.
That's why Scripture says,
"God opposes those who are proud.
But he gives grace to those who are humble."
JAMES 4:6 ESV

If you were playing a game with friends and someone got bossy, telling everyone that you had to play by their rules, how would you feel? Would you want to do it their way? Now think of someone who kindly says that there might be a better way to play the game. You would probably listen.

Jesus wants to listen to people when they ask him with a good heart. If you try to tell him to do it your way, it doesn't show that you care about what is best. Being humble means listening to Jesus. He will give you grace.

Jesus, thank you that you created me to need you. Help me to know that you always have the best way.

DOT SQUARE GAME— PLAY WITH A FRIEND!

Connect two flowers with a line. Take turns connecting flowers. If you draw a line that completes a box, put your initials in that box—it's yours! Whenever a player makes a box, they get to take another turn. At the end of the game, count the boxes with your initials in it. The player with the most boxes wins!

REWARDS WITH WORK

We believe it is through the grace of our Lord Jesus that we are saved.
ACTS 15:11 NIV

Do you get rewards for doing good things and working hard? Do you get stars on your chart, special time with your parents, or maybe even money?

Rewards are great, but that's not how you get into heaven. You don't have to do anything to be accepted by God; you just have to believe in Jesus. It can seem a little too easy, but that is what God's grace is all about. It's his gift to you.

Thank you, Jesus, that I don't have to be perfect all the time to have eternal life with you.

Word Scramble

Rearrange the letters to create words related to Easter.

RIFISECAC _ _ _ _ _ _ _ _ _

SEOTRCRRUEIN _ _ _ _ _ _ _ _ _ _ _ _

ERMOFED _ _ _ _ _ _ _

RNEIS _ _ _ _ _

ERCAG _ _ _ _ _

RVGOFIEN _ _ _ _ _ _ _ _

AIVTLANSO _ _ _ _ _ _ _ _ _

RSCOS _ _ _ _ _

MYCER _ _ _ _ _

DESINKNS _ _ _ _ _ _ _ _

Answer on page 127

FREE TO LIVE

We have freedom now because Christ made us free. So stand strong. Do not change and go back into the slavery of the law.

GALATIANS 5:1 ICB

Imagine if you had been captured and sent to jail. It would make you so happy if someone found a way to rescue you and get you out of jail. You would run free and never go near the jail again.

Jesus rescued us from our sin and we have a brand new start because he has forgiven us. When we keep feeling guilty about our sin, it's like going back to the jail and putting the chains back on our hands and feet. God wants us to feel free and good about his forgiveness, so stay free!

Jesus, thank you for giving me a brand new life in you. Thank you for freeing me from guilt and giving me a life full of grace.

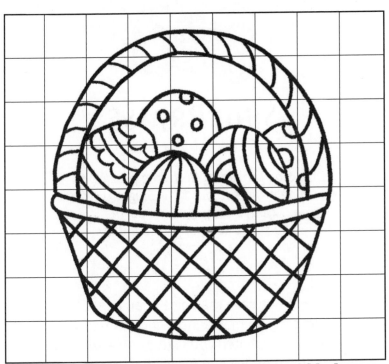

Recreate the picture above in the grid below.

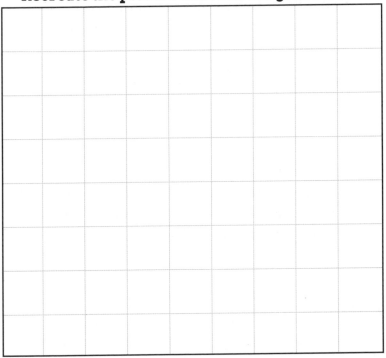

SING PRAISE

Sing praises to God. Sing praises.
Sing praises to our King. Sing praises.
God is King of all the earth.
So sing a song of praise to him.
PSALM 47:6-7 ICB

You might not have the voice of an angel, but you can sing, no matter how good or bad it sounds. God created you with a voice and with lips that can praise him for all the good things he has done. God will have so much joy by your song of praise to him - it is the most beautiful thing that he can hear!

Sing praises to God. Sing, because he is good. Sing, because you understand his grace. Sing, because he is worthy!

God, you are the king of all the earth. You have been good to me. Help me to sing and speak of your goodness!

Circle the two pictures that are exactly the same.

Answer on page 127

CHASED BY GRACE

*Surely your goodness and love will be with me
all my life.
And I will live in the house of the Lord forever.*
PSALM 23:6 ICB

We leave footprints as we walk in the sand or
mud. Have you ever trailed mud into the house
and made your parents upset with you because
of the mess?

God wants you to walk in the right direction. He
doesn't want you to walk where there is sin. That
would be like walking in dirt. The more you know
about God, the more you will understand how to
be loving and good like he is. The only footprints
you will leave then are the ones that follow Jesus,
right into his house!

**Heavenly Father, help me to follow you
as you walk beside me with goodness
and grace. Lead me to dwell in your
house forever.**

Start here

End here

85

SHINY AND NEW

Anyone who belongs to Christ has become a new
person. The old life is gone; a new life has begun!
2 CORINTHIANS 5:17 NLT

Have you ever seen a very dirty car go through
a car wash and come out sparkling clean? When
we accept Jesus into our hearts, he forgets all the
bad, ugly things we have done, and he makes us
shiny and new—like that nice clean car.

We all have bad things we would like to forget,
like mean words we've said and people we've
hurt. Every day, we can tell Jesus we are sorry for
our sin and he washes that yucky dirt away.

God, I'm so happy that you can take
my sin away. Thank you for forgiving
me and making me clean.

*C*hange one letter at a time to create new words and turn **DEAD** into **LIFE**.

D E A D

_ _ _ _ to go first

_ _ _ _ a burden

_ _ _ _ a master

_ _ _ _ an old tradition

_ _ _ _ to tempt

_ _ _ _ steady

_ _ _ _ a person of importance

_ _ _ _ a thin cable

_ _ _ _ female spouse

L I F E

Answer on page 127

WHITE AS SNOW

"Come, let's talk this over", says the Lord; "No matter how deep the stain of your sins, I can take it out and make you as clean as freshly fallen snow. Even if you are stained as red as crimson, I can make you white as wool!"
ISAIAH 1:18 TLB

When we play outside, our clothes and shoes can get really dirty. Imagine wearing really white shoes and then stepping in mud. Yuck! That mud is like sin. God said that no sin is too bad that he can't take it away.

It's a beautiful picture. If you have told Jesus that you are sorry, you are perfectly clean. If not, don't wait another moment! Talk it over with God, and be washed clean today. All you have to do is ask.

Thank you, God, that you forgive me and make me as clean as fresh snow!

COLLECT ALL THE EGGS!

Draw a line from the beginning to the end that passes through each box with an egg in it once. The line can go up, down, left, or right, but cannot go diagonal.

Start here

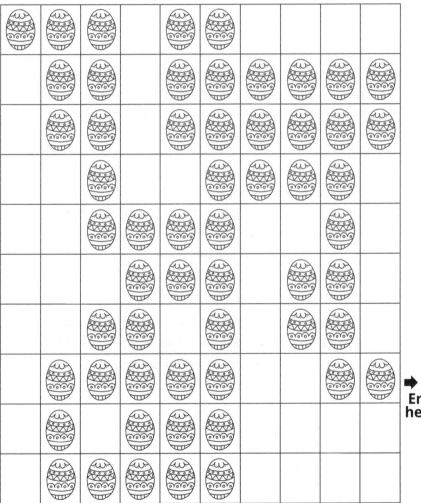

End here

SET FREE

*Live as free people, but do not use your freedom
as an excuse to do evil. Live as servants of God.*
1 PETER 2:16 NCV

When prisoners are set free, everyone expects
them to stop doing the bad things they were
doing before. When we are set free because of
Jesus, God expects us to stop doing bad things
too.

The devil doesn't want us to be close to God,
but we must fight back. Take a stand against the
enemy with prayer and God's Word, fighting for
freedom with Jesus at your side.

**Thank you, Jesus, for setting me free
from sin. Help me to be strong against
sin and keep serving you.**

Write down a word in each of the blanks below.
Use your words to create a new story.

1. _____ Adjective
2. _____ Place
3. _____ Number
4. _____ Noun (plural)
5. _____ Adjective
6. _____ Noun (plural)
7. _____ Verb (command)
8. _____ Verb (past tense)
9. _____ Place
10. _____ Number

11. _____ Place
12. _____ Number
13. _____ Verb (+ING)
14. _____ Adverb
15. _____ Adverb
16. _____ Color
17. _____ Body part (plural)
18. _____ Noun
19. _____ Adjective

EASTER SURPRISE

I was so __1__ . It was finally Easter! A big group of kids all gathered together on the __2__ to start the Easter egg hunt. There were __3__ kids all looking to collect as many __4__ as possible. I was given a __5__ basket to put my __6__ in.

On your mark, get set, __7__ ! We all __8__ off in different directions. The first place I looked was in the __9__ . I found __10__ eggs there. Next, I headed over to the __11__ . No luck there. I searched for almost __12__ minutes. The timer sounded, telling us it was time to stop __13__ eggs. My basket was __14__ full.

I sat down and __15__ opened the __16__ egg. I couldn't believe my __17__ ! Do you know what was in that egg? A __18__ ! It was the __19__ gift I have ever found in an egg.

STUCK IN THE MUD

Jesus said to the Jews who believed in him, "If you continue to obey my teaching, you are truly my followers. Then you will know the truth. And the truth will make you free."
JOHN 8:31-32 ICB

Do you know the game called "Stuck in the Mud" or "Freeze Tag"? When you get tagged, you have to freeze, and you can't move until another player sets you free by going through your legs!

Jesus said that his truth sets you free. It's kind of like we are stuck in sin and then the truth of Jesus' forgiveness sets us free. That's pretty good news, right?

Lord, fill my mind with the truth of your forgiveness that will set me free.

Figure out the secret message by using the code.

◎	🙎	☼	□	💧	✓	❖	◆	✿	✝	☺	✎	〰
A	B	C	D	E	F	G	H	I	J	K	L	M

★	↑	↓	●	⌘	❀	✕	⁂	▣	✺	✂	✖	❄
N	O	P	Q	R	S	T	U	V	W	X	Y	Z

□↑ ★↑✕ 🙎💧 ◎✎◎⌘〰💧□

✖↑⁂ ❀💧💧☺ ✝💧❀⁂❀ ↑✓ ★◎❄◎⌘💧✕◆

✺◆↑ ✺◎❀ ☼⌘⁂☼✿✓✿💧□

◆💧↑ ◆◎❀ ⌘✿❀💧★ ◆💧 ✿❀ ★↑✕ ◆💧⌘💧

❀💧💧 ✕◆💧 ↓✎◎☼💧 ✺◆💧⌘💧

✕◆💧✖ ✎◎✿□ ◆✿〰

〰◎⌘☺

__ ___ __ _____.

___ ____ ____ __ _____,

___ ___ _____.

__ ___ ____; __ __ ___ ____.

___ ___ _____ ____

____ ____ ___.

____ 16:6

Answer on page 127

Tug-of-War

"You must give your whole heart to him.
You must hold out your hands to him for help.
Put away the sin that is in your hand.
Let no evil live in your tent.
Then you can lift up your face without shame.
You can stand strong without fear."
Job 11:13-15 icb

Do you know the game tug-of-war? You and your team hold on to one end of a really big rope, and another team hold tight to the other end. You pull in different directions and try to pull the other team over the line.

At times, it feels like we are in a tug-of-war of good and bad. We want to do the right thing, and then we are pulled toward doing the wrong thing. God says that if you keep thinking about him and what he would want, it will be easier for the good side to win!

Lord, thank you that your way is the best. Help me to become stronger and stronger with you.

```
      W U M W T X U        P O I N C X L
        J Y I R U C M F    Y S I A D K S C
    S Q   N Y T L F Y D    E L T T S O K   A W
    D T P R M U I E B Q    D T E A I P M O T U
    K U E P J V P U A F    H C A R N A T I O N
    T S O T E L O I V L    N Z L R H F Z N A O
    R Z N Q G S X Z H V    Q K U I S I D A N T
    Y W Y M M I R N S Q L  D A L R S V I X I C
    Z X G R A R V Z N H W I Y Y F Z L H S V P
      K J F R I G N Y E R Q D S P H Y C M K
            F S W Q A P M O A
      O H R P L V U B E U D V D F U D Q X H
    F U U H I I H N R W F Z Q Z J F W P G A S
    N R V A E L E F J O A E L A Z A A B G R S
    G A O I C A Y L Q S H A S Y W B O D B Y V
    S P I S L C F O S I    G I V H A U T B X B
    D L B V E T T W E I    L L I L Y D P Y H B
    N V O I F R A E H F    A B Q P Y Y P C Z S
    J N   T R F I R G Y    F K I E B P F   P U
      K M U X Z J Z C      Q S L N O Y U V
      I C J S L O G        S K P J C X F
```

FIND THESE WORDS

AZALEA	IRIS	POPPY
CARNATION	LILAC	ROSE
DAFFODIL	LILY	SUNFLOWER
DAHLIA	LOTUS	TULIP
DAISY	PEONY	VIOLET

THRILL OF THE HUNT

Whoever pursues righteousness and kindness will find life and honor.
PROVERBS 21:21 NRSV

Do you like treasure hunts? Trying to find treats, money, or candy is pretty exciting! This is what it means to pursue something—to go looking and looking until you find it!

If we want to live a life that really means something, we must pursue God. We must always be looking for him and looking for all that is good and true. It's like finding the best, golden Easter egg, but it's better because we have found a life in heaven where treasures are everywhere!

Lord, I pray for your help in finding real life in you. Keep me on your path as I continue my hunt.

Circle the two pictures that are exactly the same.

Answer on page 127

Doing Good

Since future victory is sure, be strong and steady, always abounding in the Lord's work, for you know that nothing you do for the Lord is ever wasted as it would be if there were no resurrection.
1 Corinthians 15:58 TLB

When you decide to share your cookie with your sister, when you help your dad set the table, when you stop to give a teammate a hand—God notices. He notices all the good things you do, even if they seem small.

The Bible says that nothing that you do for God is ever wasted, because doing good things always shows others that there is love is the world, and this gives us all hope.

Jesus, sometimes I wonder if anyone notices some of the kind and right things that I do. Thank you that you do.

Recreate the picture above in the grid below.

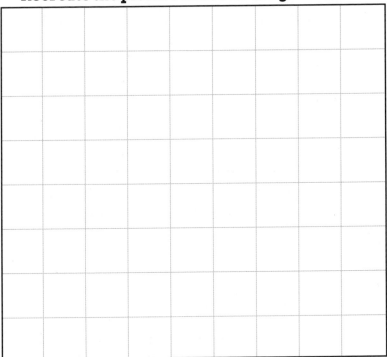

ROCK SOLID

"The rain came down, the streams rose, and the winds blew and beat against that house; yet it did not fall, because it had its foundation on the rock."
MATTHEW 7:25 NIV

Sometimes life is like a huge storm. It beats down, tosses you around, and carries you away in a flood of troubles and worries. It seems like bad stuff happens all at once. When bad things happen, who do you run to?

The Bible says that the best way to make sure you can stand tall in a storm is to know about God and to have faith in his promises. Then you will be like a house that has a strong foundation and will not break in a storm.

Lord Jesus, I know that no matter what I face, I will not fall if you are with me. I choose to believe this today.

ACROSS

4. The name of the governor at the time of Jesus' trial
7. How many days Jesus was in the tomb
8. What Jesus and his disciples ate for breakfast after his resurrection
9. What the crown placed on Jesus' head was made of
10. What people laid on the ground for Jesus' donkey to walk on (2 words, 4-8)

DOWN

1. Where the disciples met Jesus after he rose
2. What Jesus washed at the Last Supper
3. The name of the hill where the cross was located
5. The prisoner who the crowd asked to be released
6. The name of the holiday Jesus and his disciples were celebrating at the Last Supper

Answer on page 128

Best Treasures

Since you became alive again, so to speak, when Christ arose from the dead, now set your sights on the rich treasures and joys of heaven where he sits beside God in the place of honor and power. Let heaven fill your thoughts; don't spend your time worrying about things down here.
Colossians 3:1-2 TLB

Everyone around us seems to care about clothes and movies and toys. It is hard not to want to think about that all the time too.

The best treasures, though, are in heaven. That's what God wants us to think about more than things on earth. So be careful what you watch, and look at, and think about. Keep your mind on God and his Word.

Father, please help me turn away from the things of this world, and set my heart on heaven.

DOT SQUARE GAME— PLAY WITH A FRIEND!

Connect two flowers with a line. Take turns connecting flowers.
If you draw a line that completes a box, put your initials in that
box—it's yours! Whenever a player makes a box, they get to take
another turn. At the end of the game, count the boxes with your
initials in it. The player with the most boxes wins!

Circle the 10 differences between these 2 pictures, and then color!

Out of the Gates

"If the Son sets you free, you will be free indeed."
JOHN 8:36 NIV

During school, you are not allowed to leave the gates that go around the outside of the school. Once school is finished, you can walk right out of those gates without getting into trouble.

Before Jesus died and rose again, we were like kids inside a school with strict rules. When Jesus died and rose again, it was like we were let out of the gates—we were set free!

Thank you, Jesus, for rescuing me and setting me free.

New Life

"What I'm about to tell you is true. Unless a grain of wheat falls to the ground and dies, it remains only one seed. But if it dies, it produces many seeds."
John 12:24 NIRV

Have you ever seen a gigantic tree and wondered how it got so big? Have you ever thought about how that tree began? It started as a tiny seed that had fallen from another tree.

Jesus used this picture to describe what happened when he died. He fell to the ground like that tiny seed, but something so incredible happened after he died and rose again. He saved people from sin, and now we have eternal life in him. Amazing!

Thank you, Jesus, for loving me enough to die for me. In that place, new life begins. Thank you for bringing me to new life!

Start here

Find your way through the Cross

End here

HOPE IN HIS WORD

You are my hiding place and my shield;
I hope in your word.
PSALM 119:114 NCV

Hope means looking forward to something and getting excited about what is coming. Have you ever felt that way about reading the Bible?

God protects us and wants what is best for us, so he gave us the Bible full of promises. We can always go to it if we start to wonder about things or want strength or courage or love—because God and his truth are there.

Father, thank you for giving us the Bible. I pray that I would find hope and peace in your Word.

Break the code to figure out the secret message. Some of the numbers have been provided to help you get started.

		13		16					26	11		
A	B	C	D	E	F	G	H	I	J	K	L	M
8	17		22		21					25		24
N	O	P	Q	R	S	T	U	V	W	X	Y	Z

10-16-13-2-3-2-16 17-20 15-9-16 14-17-1-6-21

_ _ _ _ _ _ _   _ _   _ _ _   _ _ _ _ _

4-1-16-2-15 14-17-12-16 5-16 2-1-16 8-17-15

_ _ _ _ _   _ _ _ _   _ _   _ _ _   _ _ _

13-17-8-21-3-19-16-6 20-17-1 9-18-21

_ _ _ _ _ _ _ _   _ _ _   _ _ _

13-17-19-23-2-21-21-18-17-8-21 8-16-12-16-1 20-2-18-14

_ _ _ _ _ _ _ _ _ _ _   _ _ _ _ _   _ _ _ _

15-9-16-7 2-1-16 8-16-5 16-12-16-1-7 19-17-1-8-18-8-4

_ _ _ _   _ _ _   _ _ _   _ _ _ _ _   _ _ _ _ _ _ _

4-1-16-2-15 18-21 7-17-3-1 20-2-18-15-9-20-3-14-8-16-21-21

_ _ _ _ _   _ _   _ _ _ _   _ _ _ _ _ _ _ _ _ _ _ _.

14-2-19-16-8-15-2-15-18-17-8-21

_ _ _ _ _ _ _ _ _ _ _ _

Answer on page 128

FAITHFUL WITHOUT FAIL

Let us hold firmly to the hope that we have confessed. We can trust God to do what he promised.
HEBREWS 10:23 ICB

It can be disappointing when we have plans and then for some reason they don't happen. Maybe your friend couldn't come over to your house because they got sick, or your family was planning to go to the beach and it started to rain. Sometimes people just don't show up when they said they would!

God is not like any of these situations. The Bible says that he is faithful which means that he always, always, always does what he has promised. You can trust in him.

Lord, I pray I'd always remember you and the promises you have made. My hope is in you.

DESIGN AND COLOR
YOUR OWN EGG

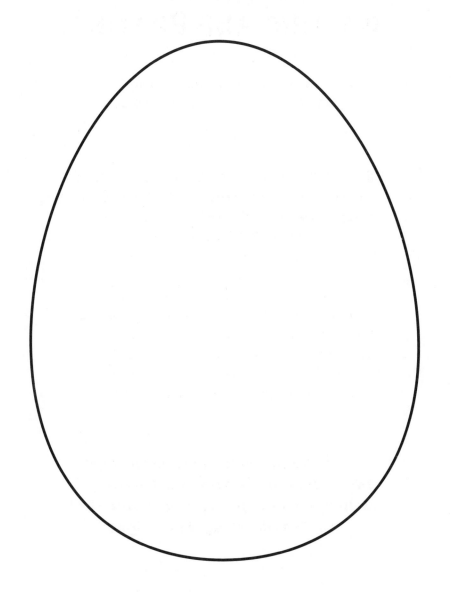

WAITING AND PRAYING

Rejoice in our confident hope.
Be patient in trouble, and keep on praying.
ROMANS 12:12 NLT

Have you ever gone to an amusement park and had to wait in line for a really long time to get on a ride? Maybe you have been to a movie and had to wait a while before it started. It can be hard to wait!

God has promised that one day he will make everything right on earth again. We will have a new heaven and a new earth and there will be no more trouble. But we have to wait! Can you wait patiently? The Bible says to be patient and to keep on praying, because it will happen!

Lord, thank you that you plan great things for our lives and for this world. Help me to keep praying, knowing that you are planning it just right.

```
                        E
                     L  S  E
                  O  Y  A  L  X
               Z  N  D  S  O  P  Q
            P  Z  H  T  R  P  F  V  V
         U  D  M  P  A  E  D  R  M  R  N
      G  H  X  G  B  M  E  A  R  W  R  C  U
   G  Y  O  X  L  L  L  A  T  A  N  J  Y  G  A
L  A  H  E  O  T  E  T  T  E  P  U  C  R  O  P  N
E  Q  Y  J  G  O  S  R  J  M  C  B  I  Z  F  O  G  H  L
F  N  N  X  Y  Q  Z  J  O  K  I  T  E  A  R  B  O  P  V  E  G
   N  B  L        L  W  E              H  P  I
   C  A  K        G  X  K              A  X  I
   U  B  I        U  N  E              T  T  Y
   P  O  D        D  A  I              C  X  Q
   C  B  T  N  E  W  G  G  A  L  M  O  H  J  C
   A  D  G  N  I  L  G  D  E  L  F  T  L  O  C
   Y  V  O  S  E  R  D  U  U  J  A  K  I  I  W
   I  Y  S  T  N  L        S  J  V  N  J  F
   C  E  L  Y  P  Y        H  V  Y  G  M  V
   F  F  I  E  E  B        A  C  N  B  I  O
   R  W  N  M  Z  K        B  S  N  U  W  X
   O  L  G  K  P  D        D  J  U  L  T  P
   O  R  Z  D  F  G        U  N  B  Q  G  M
```

FIND THESE WORDS

BABY	FOAL	KID
BUNNY	FRY	KIT
COLT	GOSLING	PORCUPETTE
EAGLET	HATCHLING	PUGGLE
FLEDGLING	JOEY	TADPOLE

LOVE DEFINITION

Love is patient and kind. Love is not jealous, it does not brag, and it is not proud. Love is not rude, is not selfish, and does not become angry easily. Love does not remember wrongs done against it. Love takes no pleasure in evil, but rejoices over the truth. Love patiently accepts all things. It always trusts, always hopes, and always continues strong.
1 CORINTHIANS 13:4-7 ICB

You are patient and kind. You are not jealous, you do not brag, you are not rude or selfish. You don't become angry easily, and you don't remember when people do wrong things to you. Does that sound like you?

Love is not just something you feel, but something you choose, even when you don't want to. It means putting other's needs before your own like Jesus did.

Jesus, you have shown me so much love and patience. Teach me how to love like you and help me to put others first the way you do.

COLLECT ALL THE FLOWERS!

Draw a line from the beginning to the end that passes through each box with a flower in it once. The line can go up, down, left, or right, but cannot go diagonal.

Start here ➡

➡ **End here**

CONSUMED

I have hope
when I think of this:
The Lord's love never ends.
His mercies never stop.
LAMENTATIONS 3:21-22 ICB

What is on your mind today? Are you worried about a friend? Your parents? A test at school? Sometimes we think too much about the problem and don't think enough about the answer.

The answer is always God. When we remember that God is full of love, we can be filled with hope. We can feel much better when we think about how great God is.

Holy Spirit, help me to think about your great love the next time I can only think about my problems, so that I can have hope.

Figure out the secret message by using the code.

◎	🔺	☼	□	◆	✓	❖	♦	❀	✝	☺	✏	≈
A	B	C	D	E	F	G	H	I	J	K	L	M

★	↑	↓	●	⌘	✿	✖	✳	▣	✴	✂	※	❄
N	O	P	Q	R	S	T	U	V	W	X	Y	Z

_ _ _ _ _ _ _ _ _ _' _ _ _ _ _ _ _ _

_ _ _ _ _ _ _ _ _ _ _ _ _ _ _ _ _ _ _'

_ _ _ _ _ _ _ _ _ _ _ _ _ _ _ _.

_ _ _ _ _ _ _ _ _ _ _ _'

_ _ _ _ _ _ _ _ _ _ _ _ _ _ _.

_ _ _ _ 14:19

Joyful Waiting

I wait for the Lord, my whole being waits,
and in his word I put my hope.
PSALM 130:5 NIV

Waiting for something can be very hard, and not fun at all. But sometimes waiting is exciting: waiting to tell something great, waiting for a family vacation, waiting to give someone a gift.

When we wait for good things, the waiting can be a gift too. This is how it is to wait for the Lord. We will eventually be with God forever, and waiting for that to happen is fun!

Lord, I love waiting for you. Because I know you bring only goodness, I can wait for you with hope.

Start here

ANSWERS

Pg. 7

purple, pink, green, yellow, orange, red, blue, brown, black, white

Pg. 15

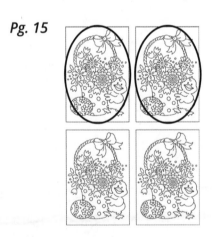

Pg. 21

sins, pins, pine, line, lint, list, gist, gift

Pg. 27

teaser, taser, tease, rates, reset, stare, steer, arts, ears, eats, rate, rats, rest, seat, seer, star, tase, teas, tees, art, eat, ear, rat, sea, see, set, tar, tea, tee

Pg. 29

Across – 1. Jesus.   3. Fast.   5. Lent.   6. Sacrifice.
8. Resurrection.
Down – 2. Easter.   4. Good Friday.   5. Last Supper.
7. Christian.   9. Tomb.

Pg. 31

chick, pony, puppy, kitten, fawn, lamb, duckling, cub, calf, piglet

Pg. 35

I know that my redeemer lives, and that in the end he will stand on the earth. Job 19:25

Pg. 43

Pg. 47

baste, beast, beats, skate, stake, steak, takes, base, bask, bats, beat, best, bets, tabs, take, task, seat, stab, ask, bat, bet, sat, sea, set, tab

Pg. 57

12	17	1	4	15	18	10	21	2	8	13	14	9
A	B	C	D	E	F	G	H	I	J	K	L	M
6	5	23	25	7	22	20	24	3	11	16	19	26
N	O	P	Q	R	S	T	U	V	W	X	Y	Z

For God so loved the world that he gave his one and only Son, that whoever believes in him shall not perish but have eternal life. John 3:16

Pg. 59

Judas, Peter, Jesus, Mary Magdalene, Simon, Pontius Pilate, disciples, John, Pharisees, James

Pg. 67

He is not here. He has risen!

Pg. 69

Across – 3. Hosanna. 7. Gethsemane. 8. Judas.
10. Peter.
Down – 1. Caiaphas. 2. Ear. 4. Bread. 5. Sleep.
6. Donkey. 9. Angel.

Pg. 79

sacrifice, resurrection, freedom, risen, grace, forgiven, salvation, cross, mercy, kindness

Pg. 83

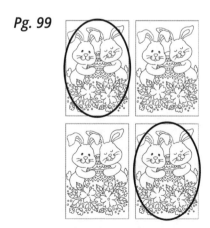

Pg. 87

dead, lead, load, lord, lore, lure, sure, sire, wire, wife, life

Pg. 95

Do not be alarmed. You seek Jesus of Nazareth, who was crucified. He has risen; he is not here. see the place where they laid him. Mark 16:6

Pg. 99

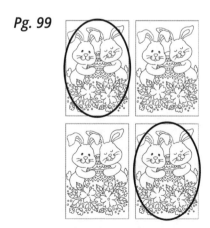

Pg. 103

Across – 4. Pilate.   7. Three.   8. Fish.   9. Thorns.
10. Palm branches.
Down – 1. Galilee.   2. Feet.   3. Golgotha.   5. Barabbas.
6. Passover.

Pg. 113

2	10	13	6	16	20	4	9	18	26	11	14	19
A	B	C	D	E	F	G	H	I	J	K	L	M
8	17	23	22	1	21	15	3	12	5	25	7	24
N	O	P	Q	R	S	T	U	V	W	X	Y	Z

Because of the Lord's great love we are not consumed, for
his compassions never fail. They are new every morning;
great is your faithfulness.
Lamentations 3:22-23

Pg. 121

Before long, the world will not see me anymore, but you will
see me. Because I live, you also will live. John 14:19